ILYAS & DUCK
Ramadan Joy!

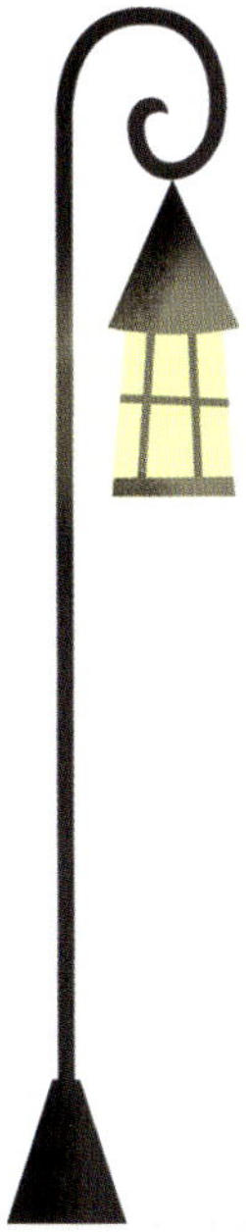

Written by Omar S. Khawaja

Illustrated by Leo Antolini

The best opportunity is the one you recognize.
Ramadan Mubarak.
- O.S.K.

Copyright © 2018 by Omar S. Khawaja
Illustrated by Leo Antolini
Edited by Minha Kauser

All rights reserved. This book, or parts thereof, may not be reproduced in any form without the permission in writing from the publisher, LBK Books, a subsidiary of Little Big Kids, LLC

LBK Books
Hatched in Washington D.C.
www.LittleBigKids.com

Printed in China
This product conforms to CPSIA 2008
First Printing, 2018

Library of Congress Control Number: 2018931827

ISBN 978-0-9850728-6-5

1 2 3 4 5 6   21 20 19 18

O you who have believed, decreed upon you is fasting as it was decreed upon those before you that you may become righteous.

- The Qur'an: Surah (chapter) 2, *verse 283*

Ilyas and Duck stood at the edge of town, patiently watching the setting sun.

Then the moon appeared and Ilyas said with cheer, "Look, Duck! Up there! I see the crescent moon!"

And just like that,
the month of Ramadan had begun.

The joy of Ramadan spread quickly through town,
with festive decorations and lanterns abound.

The smell of treats spilled into the streets,
as the baker prepared Suhoor,
the last meal before the daytime fast,
that is *so* important to eat.

Then morning came and the sun was out.

"Duck...Wait!" Ilyas had to shout.

"The sun is still up, let's not forget."
"Don't break your fast, at least not yet!"

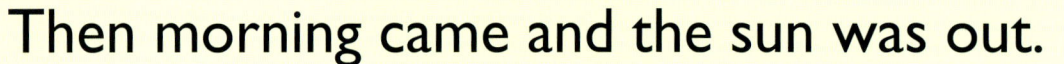

Fasting is not meant to be easy. It can leave your belly **empty** and **grumbling** inside.

But know this feeling is just Allah's way of feeding **goodness** to your **body** and **mind**.

Goodness like,

Compassion to care for the less fortunate,

Empathy to feel the hunger they often do.

Gratitude to appreciate all the blessings you have.

And a **Reminder** of just how fragile you are,

and that it's **Allah** who provides for you.

Fasting is a chance to nourish your **soul**, your relationship with **Allah** and your **community**, too.

It's a chance to practice **self-discipline** and **restraint**, and build **confidence** in all that you do.

Oh.

And so...

They broke their fast with just a few **dates,**

drank water, **prayed,**

and *then* they **ate.**

They met friends and family all around town.
And all around town not a frown could be found.

That is...until they reached the other end of town.

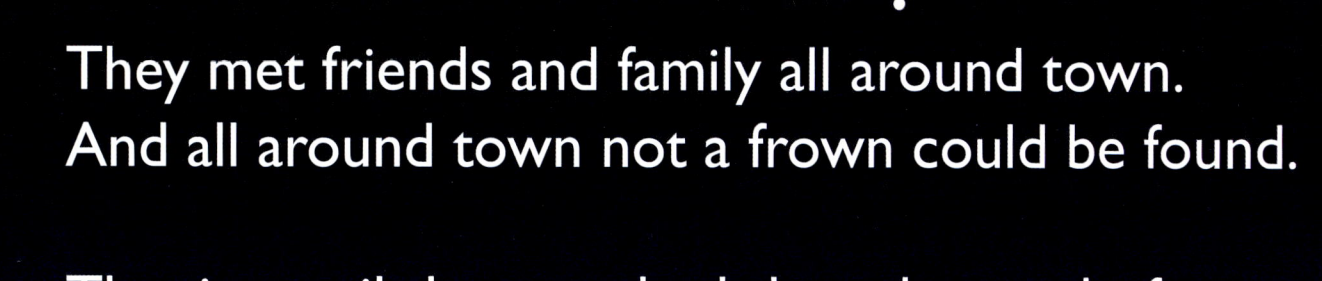

Because at the other end of town, on top of a hill, lived a man who was rarely ever seen.

No one really knew who he was and no one knew his real name but they all did know him as...

"Oh, I'm not fond of this month, Ramadan.
For 30 days, the kids are so well behaved.
For 30 days, all their bad deeds are gone.
Everyone is so kind, they give extra charity and stuff.
How will I ever stand all this goodness for 30 long days?

I know. I will spoil Ramadan! I've had enough!"

"I will cover entire neighborhoods with my menacing spray so kids may continue to play even when it's time to pray."

"I will bake mouth-watering cookies and place them all around so kids are tempted to break their fast, even before the sun goes down."

"Yes! This is how I will spoil Ramadan and make it what it's NOT meant to be!"

"Oh, no!" exclaimed Ilyas. "Mister Mean is up to no good!"

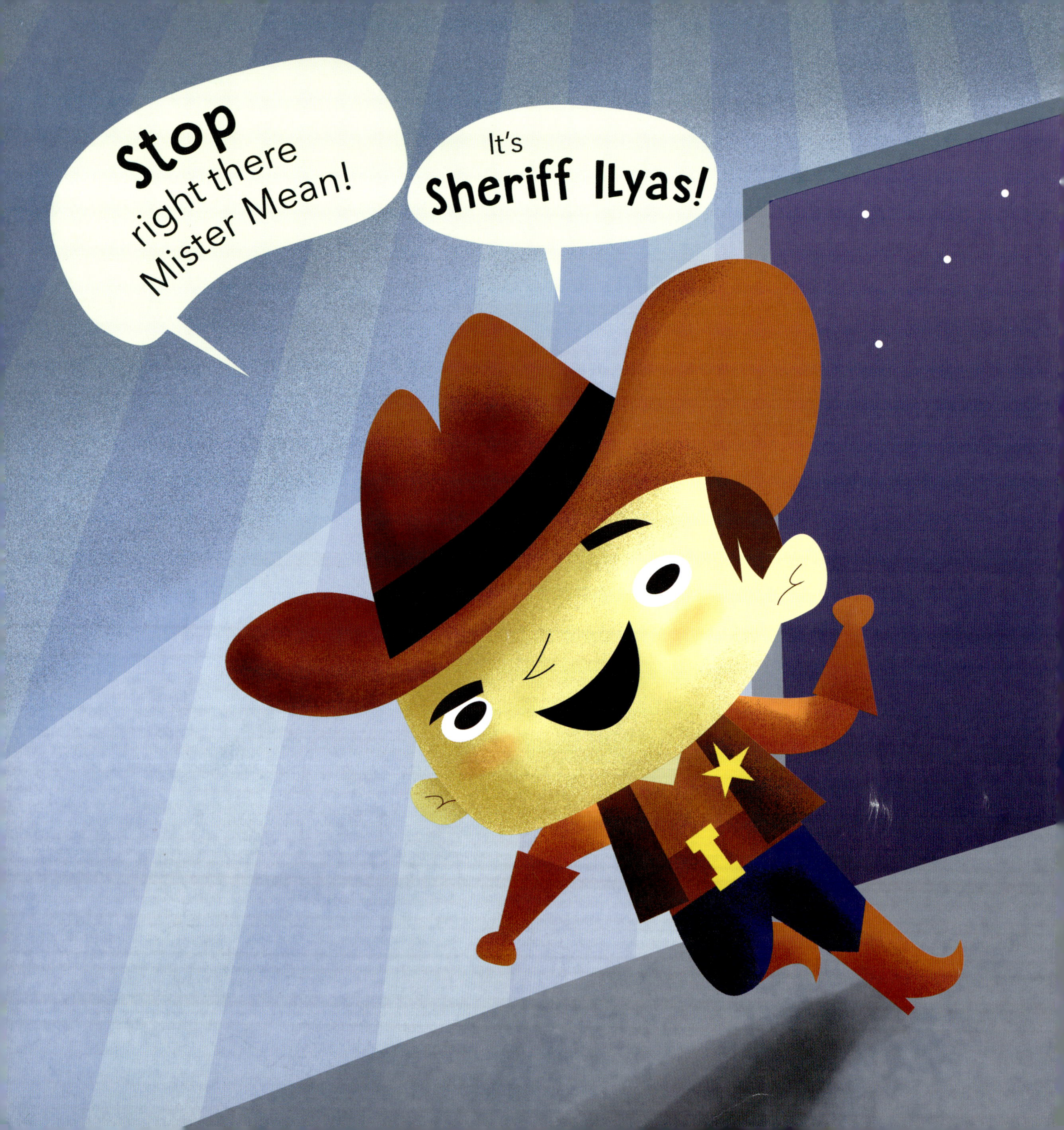
Stop right there Mister Mean!
It's Sheriff ILyas!

Mister Mean got away but it's a good thing he's gone because there's no room for meanness, only goodness in Ramadan.

And when a good deed is done, the reward for it is multiplied not just once or twice, not three times nor four, but MANY, MANY,

As the days of Ramadan passed one by one, each day's fast helped to improve everyone.

There was increased patience, better health and improved habits that were quite clear.

Indeed, each day was a chance to practice all these things and carry better habits through the rest of the year.

So, for the remainder of the month in the last ten days, Ilyas and Duck looked forward to the *rising* sun.

While they were thankful for the joy from the Ramadan days that passed, they were especially excited for all the blessings to come.

Ramadan Mubarak
Have a blessed Ramadan

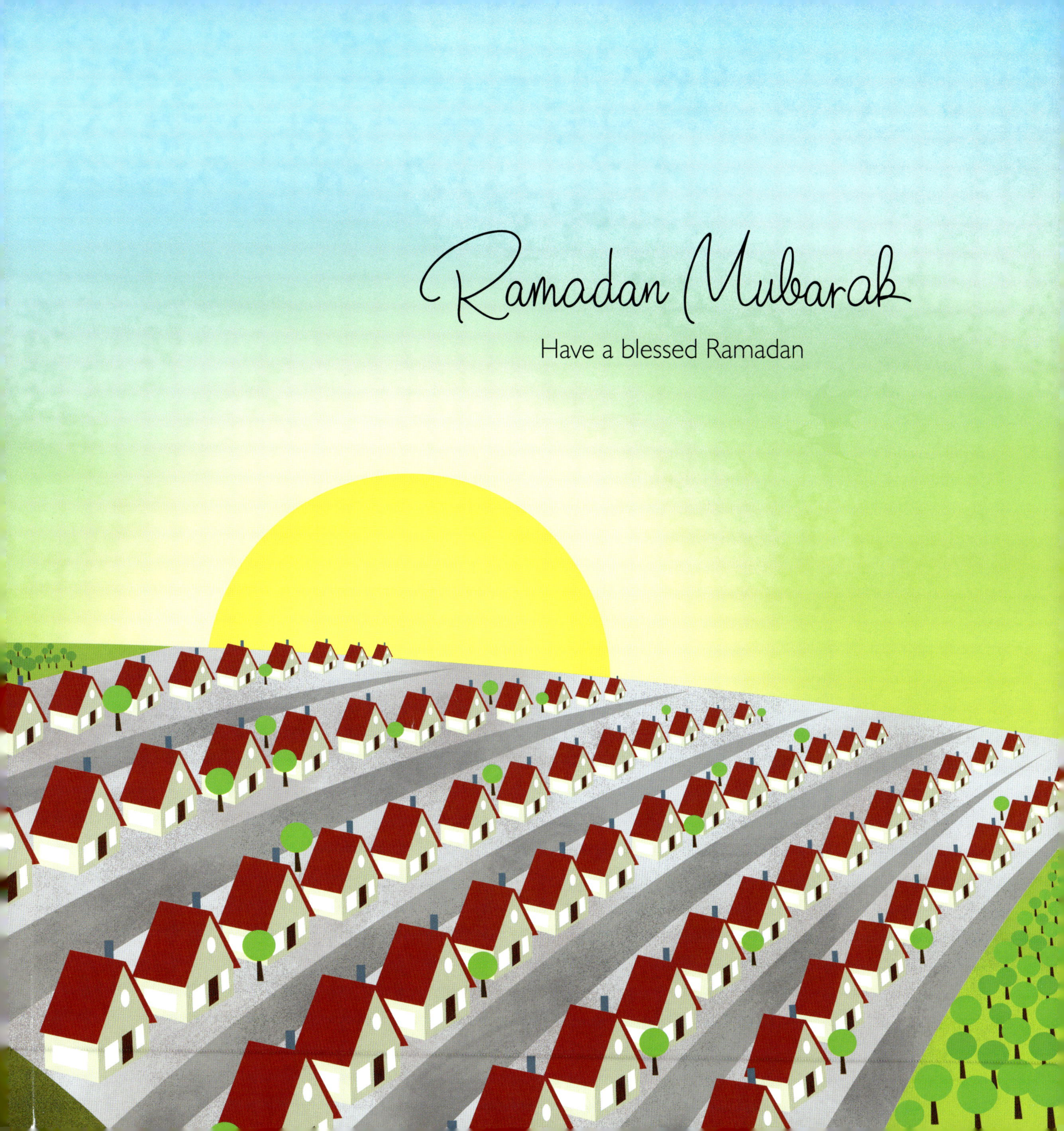

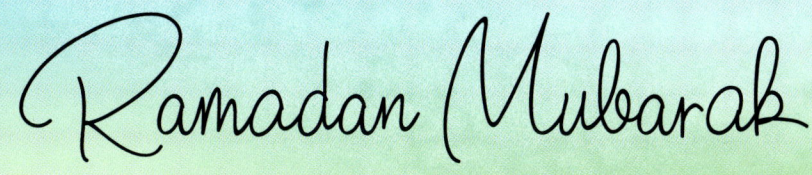

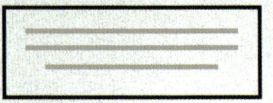 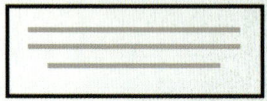

The Current Times

VOL. 1439   TODAY'S DATE, THIS YEAR

RAMADAN BEGINS!

Town prepares for the most festive and blessed time of year

Another blessed month of Ramadan is here and all the townspeople are full of joy and excitement. During Ramadan, Muslims all around the world do not eat or drink from dawn to sunset to be obedient to the will of God, gain empathy for the less fortunate and improve their habits. It's also one of the five pillars of Islam.

"I enjoy Ramadan for all the family time, festivities and food," said the baker who recently opened a bakery on West Beak Road.

"It's early in Ramadan but already good deeds have been reported all around town," said Deputy Duck. "This is great news especially since there have been increased sightings of menacing Mister Mean."

The Crescent Moon Shines Bright

The Islamic calendar consists of 12 months that are based on the orbit of the moon around the earth. Did you know this is different from what is called the Gregorian calendar that you use at your school? That calendar is based on the orbit of the earth around the sun. In the *Islamic* calendar, each new month (like Ramadan) begins when we see a thin sliver of the moon in the sky. How large the moon appears depends on how much of it is lit up by the sun. As the moon orbits Earth throughout the month, we see it grow from a thin crescent to a full disk (or full moon) and then shrink back to a thin crescent again before vanishing (new moon). Now that's science!

Ramadan Roundup!

New this Ramadan! Collectible cards for kids of all ages. This month, as you fast, do good deeds and improve your habits, you can earn these exciting and motivational cards to mark your achievements. To get your cards and collect them all, visit:
ilyasandduck.com/ramadan

Science Discovery: Fasting Is Good For Your Body

New research from the Feathers Institute for the Study of Awesome Things has concluded that fasting during Ramadan is actually good for your body. Head of Research at the Institute, Dr. Ilyas, sums up the study nicely by saying, "Fasting gives your digestive system the rest it needs to perform at its best. So I recommend that you fast and be healthy!"